Traditional & Popular
Wedding Music

Project Manager: Carol Cuellar
Cover Design: Debbie Johns Lipton
Wedding Photo: © Ron Chapple 1993, FPG International
Art Photography: Copyright ©1996 PhotoDisc, Inc. All Rights Reserved

© 1997 WARNER BROS. PUBLICATIONS
All Rights Reserved

Alphabetical Contents

Content-Category

Popular Favorites

From the Original Motion Picture Soundtrack "THE THREE MUSKETEERS"

ALL FOR LOVE

Written by
BRYAN ADAMS, ROBERT JOHN "MUTT" LANGE
and MICHAEL KAMEN

All for Love - 6 - 1

ALL THE MAN THAT I NEED

Words by
DEAN PITCHFORD

Music by
MICHAEL GORE

All the Man That I Need - 3 - 1

ALWAYS

Written by
JONATHAN LEWIS, WAYNE LEWIS
and DAVID LEWIS

Always - 3 - 1

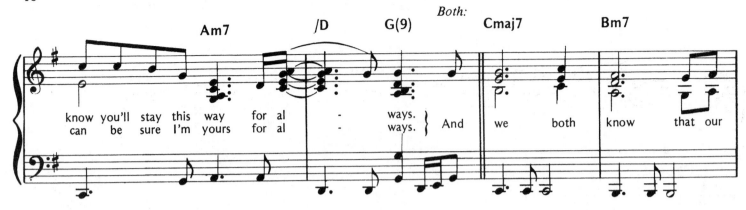

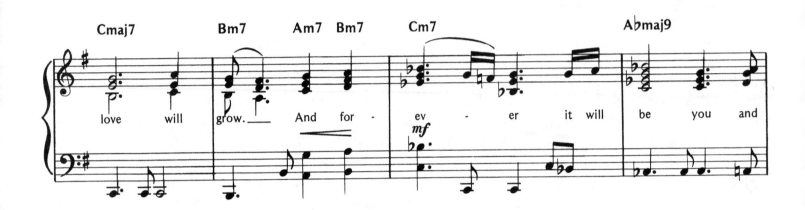

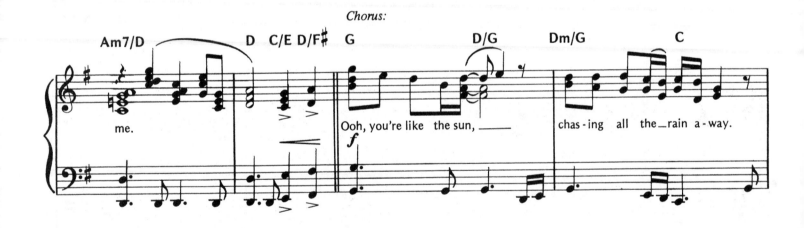

Always - 3 - 2

and you for-ev-er will be. And I will love you so for al - ways.

al - ways. Ooh, _____ ooh _____ hoo. _____

mf

Repeat ad lib. and fade

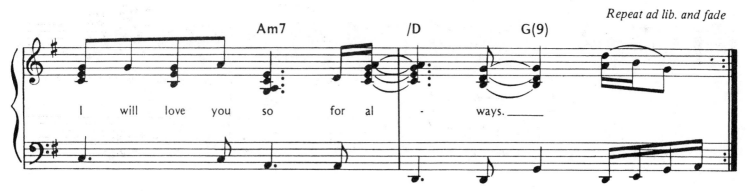

I will love you so for al - ways. _____

Always - 3 - 3

BECAUSE YOU LOVED ME
(Theme from "Up Close & Personal")

Words and Music by
DIANE WARREN

Because You Loved Me - 5 - 1

From the Columbia Picture ''THE GREATEST'' - A Columbia/EMI Presentation

THE GREATEST LOVE OF ALL

Words by
LINDA CREED

Music by
MICHAEL MASSER

I be-lieve the child—ren are the fut-ure; teach them well and let— them lead—the way.

Show them all the beau-ty they pos-sess in - side.———— Give them a

The Greatest Love Of All - 5 - 1

COUNT ON ME

Words and Music by
BABYFACE, WHITNEY HOUSTON
and MICHAEL HOUSTON

Count on Me - 6 - 1

FAITHFULLY

Slow rock ♩ = 66

Words and Music by
JONATHAN CAIN

Faithfully - 4 - 1

And lov-in' a mu-sic man__ain't al-ways what it's

s'pposed to be.__ Oh girl, you stand__ by me. I'm for-

ev-er__yours, __ faith-ful-ly. __ (Instrumental Solo)

(end solo) 2. Cir-cus

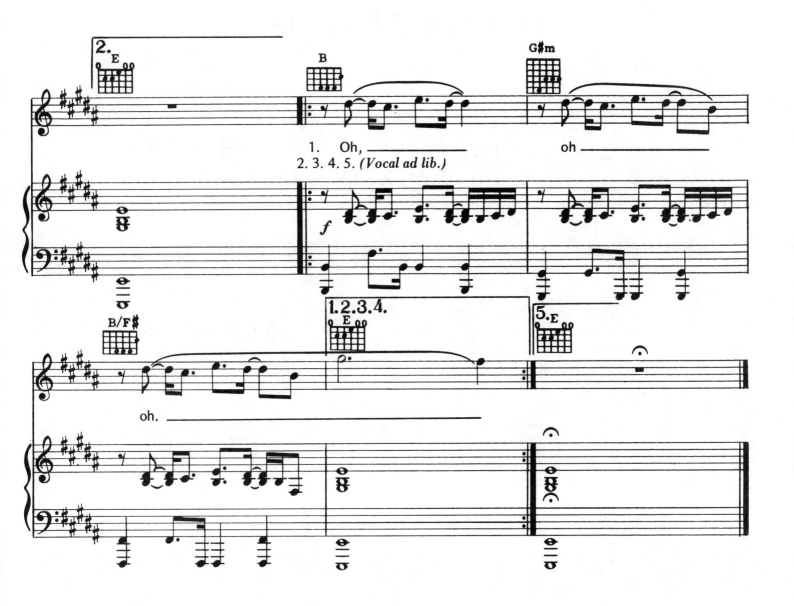

Verse 2:
Circus life
Under the big top world;
We all need the clowns
To make us smile.
Through space and time
Always another show.
Wondering where I am;
Lost without you.

And being apart ain't easy
On this love affair;
Two strangers learn to fall
In love again.
I get the joy
Of rediscovering you.
Oh girl, you stand by me.
I'm forever yours, faithfully.

Faithfully - 4 - 4

From the Twentieth Century Fox Motion Picture "ONE FINE DAY"

FOR THE FIRST TIME

Slowly ♩ = 62

Words and Music by
JAMES NEWTON-HOWARD,
ALLAN RICH and JUD FRIEDMAN

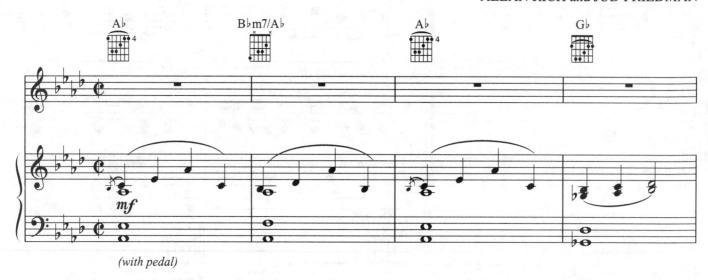

(with pedal)

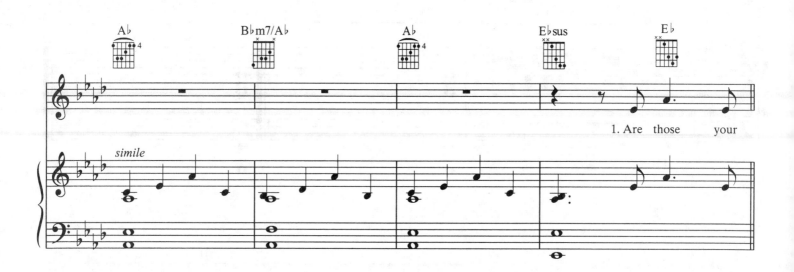

1. Are those your

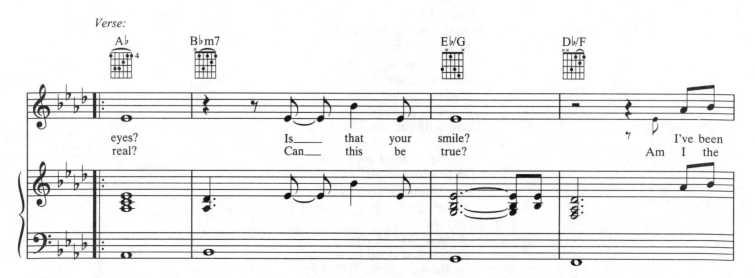

Verse:

eyes?   Is____ that your smile?   I've been
real?   Can____ this be true?   Am I the

For the First Time - 6 - 1

For the First Time - 6 - 2

Chorus:

And for the first time, I am look-ing in___ your eyes.

For the first time, I'm___ see-ing who you are.___

I can't be-lieve___ how much I see___ when you're look-ing back___ at me.___

Now I un-der-stand___ what_____ love___ is,

love_ is for the first time._____

freely

a tempo

rit.

(I Wanna Take) FOREVER TONIGHT

Words and Music by
ANDY GOLDMARK and ERIC CARMEN

(I Wanna Take) Forever Tonight - 6 - 1

ev - er to - night,___ wan - na stay___ in this mo - ment for - ev -

- er. I'm gon - na give you all the love that I've got.___ 'Cause I can't live with - out___

___ you.

Repeat ad lib. and fade

(I Wanna Take) Forever Tonight - 6 - 6

HEAVEN

Words and Music by
BRYAN ADAMS and
JIM VALLANCE

heav - en. And love is all___ that I need, and I

found it there___ in your heart. It is - n't too hard___ to see___ we're in

1.
heav-en.

D.S. %

2.
heav-en.

To next strain

3.
heav - en, heav- en.___

Repeat ad. lib. and fade

53

Heaven - 4 - 4

From the Original Soundtrack Album "THE PREACHER'S WIFE"

I BELIEVE IN YOU AND ME

Words and Music by
SANDY LINZER and DAVID WOLFERT

I Believe in You and Me - 4 - 1

Freely

I be-lieve, I do____ be-lieve in you and me. See I'm lost,____ now I'm free,____ 'cause I be-lieve__ in you__ and____ me, be-lieve__ in you____ and me.____

a tempo

rit.

Verse 2:
I will never leave your side,
I will never hurt your pride.
When all the chips are down,
I will always be around,
Just to be right where you are, my love.
Oh, I love you, boy.
I will never leave you out,
I will always let you in
To places no one has ever been.
Deep inside, can't you see?
I believe in you and me.
(To Bridge:)

From the Motion Picture "ROBIN HOOD: PRINCE OF THIEVES"

(EVERYTHING I DO) I DO IT FOR YOU

Words and Music by
BRYAN ADAMS, ROBERT JOHN "MUTT" LANGE
and MICHAEL KAMEN

(Everything I Do) I Do It for You - 4 - 1

From the Motion Picture "THE MIRROR HAS TWO FACES"

I FINALLY FOUND SOMEONE

Words and Music by
BARBRA STREISAND, MARVIN HAMLISCH,
R. J. LANGE and BRYAN ADAMS

I Finally Found Someone - 8 - 1

64

I LOVE YOU ALWAYS FOREVER

Words and Music by
DONNA LEWIS

"I LOVE YOU ALWAYS FOREVER" is inspired by the H.E. Bates Novel "LOVE FOR LYDIA."
Chorus/Bridge lyric courtesy of MICHAEL JOSEPH LTD. and THE ESTATE OF H.E. BATES.

I Love You Always Forever - 5 - 2

72

Verse 3:
You've got the most unbelievable blue eyes I've ever seen.
You've got me almost melting away as we lay there
Under blue sky with pure white stars,
Exotic sweetness, a magical time.
(To Chorus:)

OPEN ARMS

Words and Music by
STEVE PERRY and JONATHAN CAIN

Verse:

1. Ly - ing____ be - side__ you, here in____ the dark; feel - ing your
2. Soft - ly____ you whis - per, you're so____ sin - cere. How could our
3.4.*(see additional lyrics)*

heart beat with mine.
love be so blind?____

1. We
2.*(see additional lyrics)*

Open Arms - 3 - 1

76

Open Arms - 3 - 2

Verse 3:
Living without you; living alone,
This empty house seems so cold.

Verse 4:
Wanting to hold you, wanting you near;
How much I wanted you home.

Bridge:
But now that you've come back;
Turned night into day;
I need you to stay.
(Chorus)

Open Arms - 3 - 3

From the Twentieth Century-Fox Motion Picture "THE ROSE"

THE ROSE

Words and Music by
AMANDA McBROOM

The Rose - 4 - 1

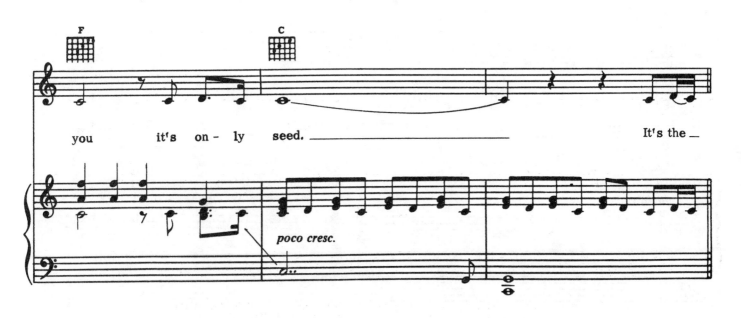

The Rose - 4 - 2

soul ... a- fraid of dy - in' that nev - er _____ learns to

seed ... that with the sun's _____ love in the

live. _____ When the _____

spring be - comes the rose.

play 3 times

rit . . . .

From the TriStar Pictures Feature Film "ONLY YOU"

ONCE IN A LIFETIME

Words and Music by
WALTER AFANASIEFF, MICHAEL BOLTON
and DIANE WARREN

1.Some peo-ple fill___ their lives___ with emp-ty nights___ and days___ that slip a-way.___
2.Some peo-ple live___ their lives___ in com-pro-mise___ and hide___ their dreams a-way.___

Once in a Lifetime - 6 - 1

From the Columbia Picture "ICE CASTLES"

THEME FROM ICE CASTLES

(Through the Eyes of Love)

Lyrics by CAROLE BAYER SAGER   Music by MARVIN HAMLISCH

Theme From Ice Castles - 3 - 1

now I do be-lieve that e-ven in the storm we'll find _____ some

light. Know - ing you're be - side me I'm all__ right. _____

D.S. al Coda

Coda

through the eyes _____ of love.

Theme From Ice Castles - 3 - 3

TIME IN A BOTTLE

Words and Music by
JIM CROCE

Time in a Bottle - 3 - 1

WE'VE ONLY JUST BEGUN

Lyric by
PAUL WILLIAMS

Music by
ROGER NICHOLS

We've Only Just Begun - 3 - 1

WHEN A MAN LOVES A WOMAN

Words and Music by
CALVIN LEWIS and ANDREW WRIGHT

When a Man Loves a Woman - 5 - 1

From the Original Motion Picture Soundtrack "BEACHES"

THE WIND BENEATH MY WINGS

Words and Music by
LARRY HENLEY and JEFF SILBAR

The Wind beneath My Wings - 7 - 1

The Wind beneath My Wings - 7 - 2

The Wind beneath My Wings - 7 - 4

The Wind beneath My Wings - 7 - 6

YOU ARE SO BEAUTIFUL

Words and Music by
BILLY PRESTON and
BRUCE FISHER

You Are So Beau-ti-ful ___ to ___ me.

(Instr. 2nd time)

You Are So Beau-ti-ful ___ to ___

You Are So Beautiful - 3 - 1

You Are So Beautiful - 3 - 3

YOU ARE THE SUNSHINE OF MY LIFE

Words and Music by
STEVIE WONDER

Moderately, with feeling

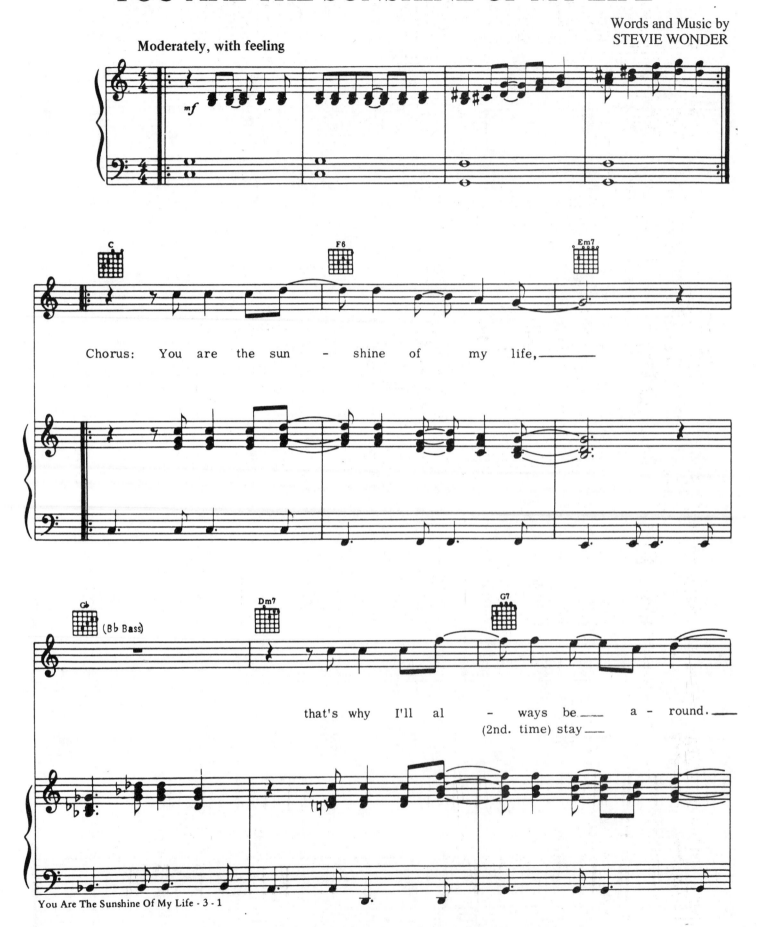

Chorus: You are the sun - shine of my life,____

that's why I'll al - ways be____ a - round.____
(2nd. time) stay____

You Are The Sunshine Of My Life - 3 - 1

You Are The Sunshine Of My Life - 3 - 3

YOU MEAN THE WORLD TO ME

By L.A. REID,
DARYL SIMMONS and BABYFACE

You Mean the World to Me - 5 - 1

118

You Mean the World to Me - 5 - 4

Country Favorites

FOREVER'S AS FAR AS I'LL GO

Words and Music by
MIKE REID

mit I could feel it the first time that we touched.__ The look in__ your eyes__

said you felt__ as much.__ But I'm not a man__ who falls so eas - i - ly.__

Forever's As Far As I'll Go - 3 - 1

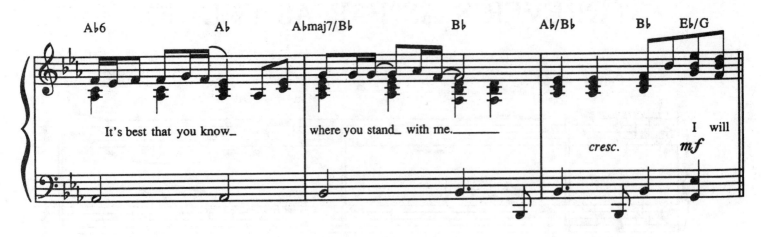

It's best that you know___ where you stand__ with me._____ cresc. I will

Chorus:

give you my heart_____ faith - ful__ and true,__ and all the love it can hold_____

that's all I can do.__ But I've thought a - bout_____ how long I'll__ love you,

and it's on - ly fair that you know,_____ for - ev - er's__ as far__ as__ I__

Verse 2:
When there's age around my eyes and gray in your hair,
And it only takes a touch to recall the love we've shared.
I won't take for granted that you know my love is true.
Each night in your arms, I will whisper to you...
(To Chorus:)

Forever's As Far As I'll Go - 3 - 3

ANGELS AMONG US

Words and Music by
BECKY HOBBS and DON GOODMAN

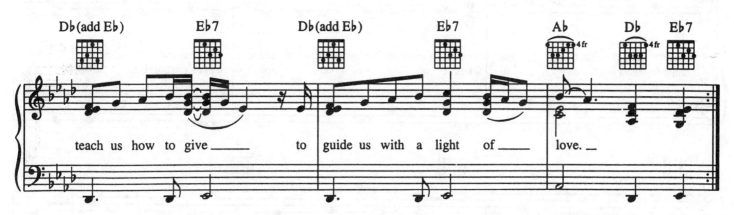

Additional lyrics

When life held troubled times and had me down on my knees,
There's always been someone to come along and comfort me.
A kind word from a stranger, to lend a helping hand,
A phone call from a friend just to say I understand.
Now, ain't it kind of funny, at the dark end of the road,
Someone lights the way with just a single ray of hope.

(To Chorus)

I CAN LOVE YOU LIKE THAT

Words and Music by
STEVE DIAMOND, MARIBETH DERRY
and JENNIFER KIMBALL

I Can Love You Like That - 4 - 1

I CROSS MY HEART

Words and Music by
STEVE DORFF and
ERIC KAZ

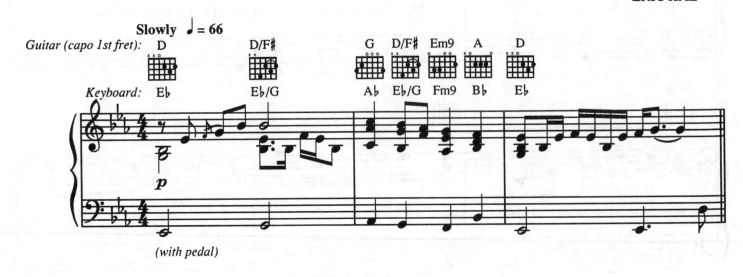

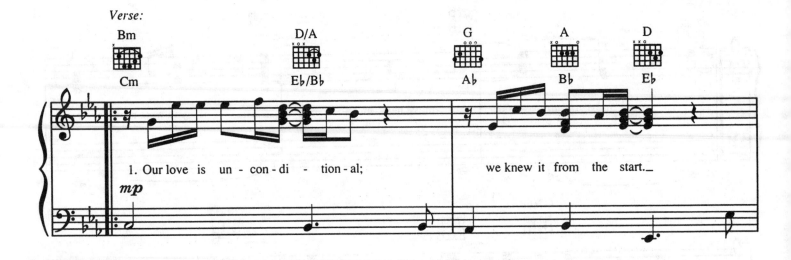

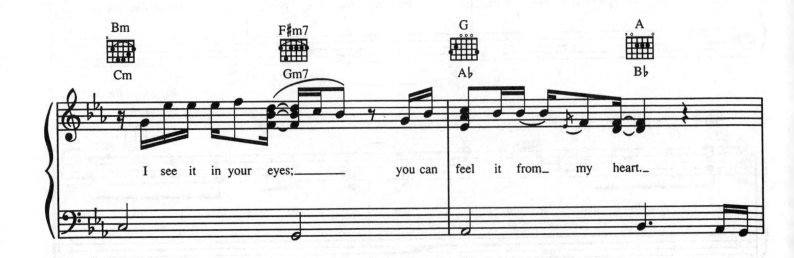

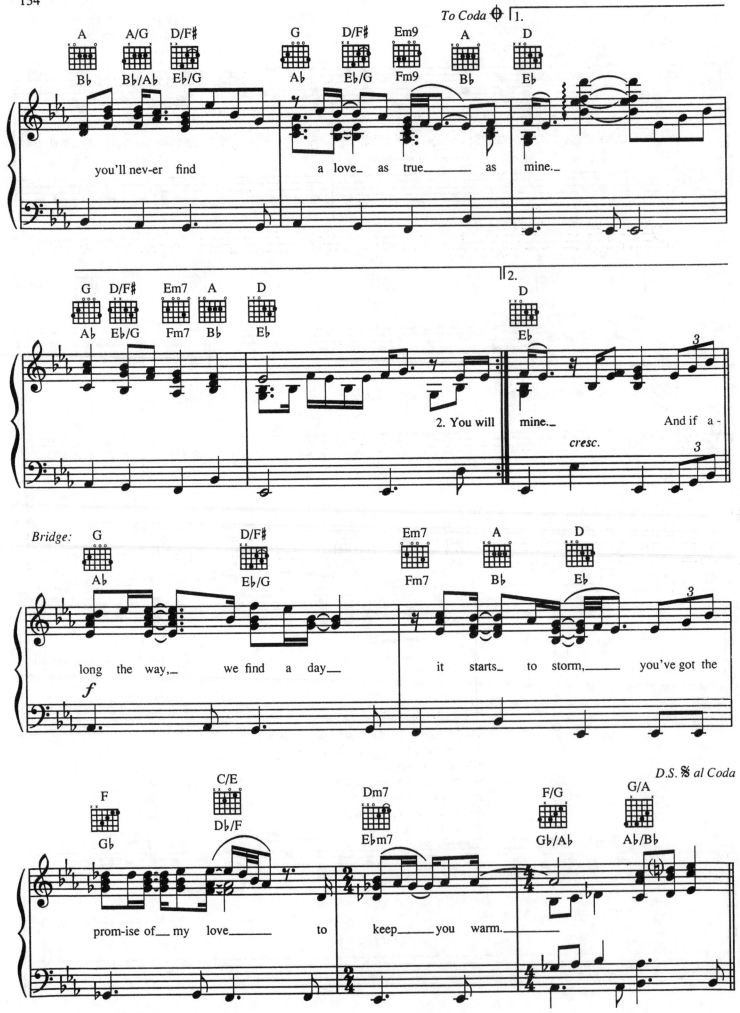

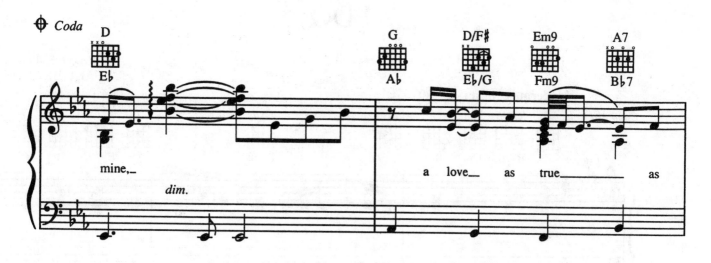

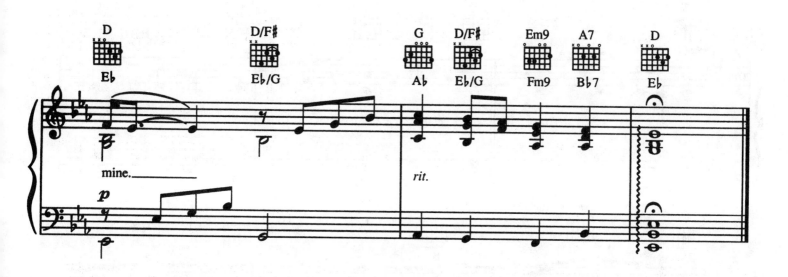

Verse 2:
You will always be the miracle
That makes my life complete;
And as long as there's a breath in me,
I'll make yours just as sweet.
As we look into the future,
It's as far as we can see,
So let's make each tomorrow
Be the best that it can be.
(To Chorus:)

I DO

Words and Music by
PAUL BRANDT

I Do - 4 - 1

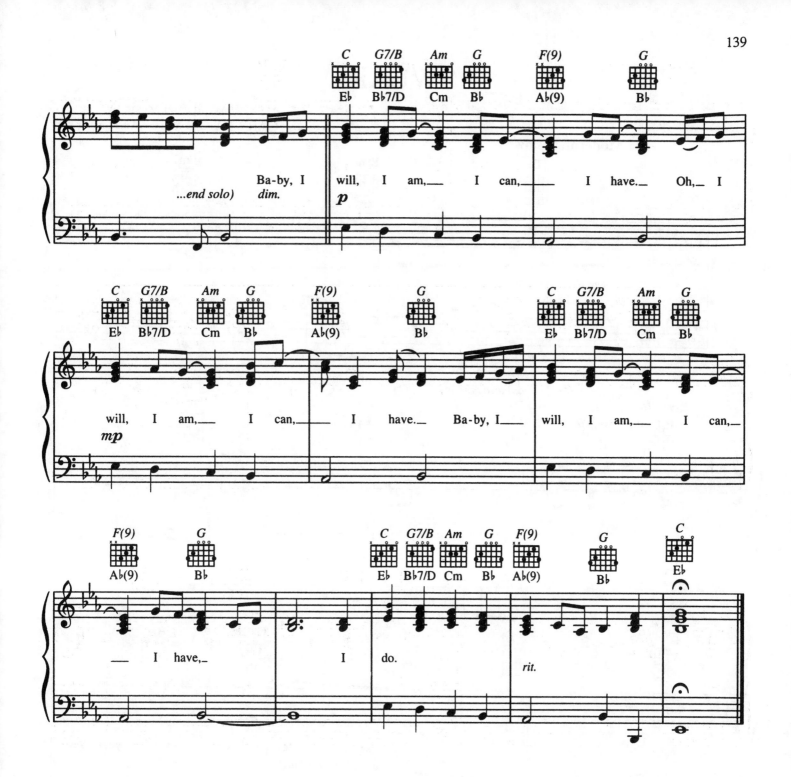

Verse 3:
I know the time will disappear,
But this love we're building on will always be here.
No way that this is sinking sand,
On this solid rock we'll stand forever...
(To Chorus:)

I SWEAR

Words and Music by
GARY BAKER and FRANK MYERS

I Swear - 4 - 1

Additional lyrics

2. I'll give you everything I can,
   I'll build your dreams with these two hands,
   And we'll hang some memories on the wall.
   And when there's silver in your hair,
   You won't have to ask if I still care,
   'Cause as time turns the page my love won't age at all.
   (To Chorus)

IN THIS LIFE

Words and Music by
MIKE REID and
ALLEN SHAMBLIN

In This Life - 3 - 1

Verse 2:
For every mountain I have climbed.
Every raging river crossed,
You were the treasure that I longed to find.
Without your love I would be lost.
(To Chorus:)

ME AND YOU

Words and Music by
SKIP EWING and RAY HERNDON

Me and You - 3 - 1

Verse 5:
Ordinary?
No, really don't think so.
Just a precious few
Ever make it last,
Get as lucky as
Me and you.

THE KEEPER OF THE STARS

Words and Music by
KAREN STALEY, DANNY MAYO and DICKIE LEE

Slowly ♩ = 76

(with pedal)

Verse:

1. It was no ac - ci - dent,
2. Soft moon-light on your face,

me find - ing
oh how you

you.
shine!

Some-one had a hand in it
It takes my breath a - way

long be - fore we ev - er knew.
just to look in - to your eyes.

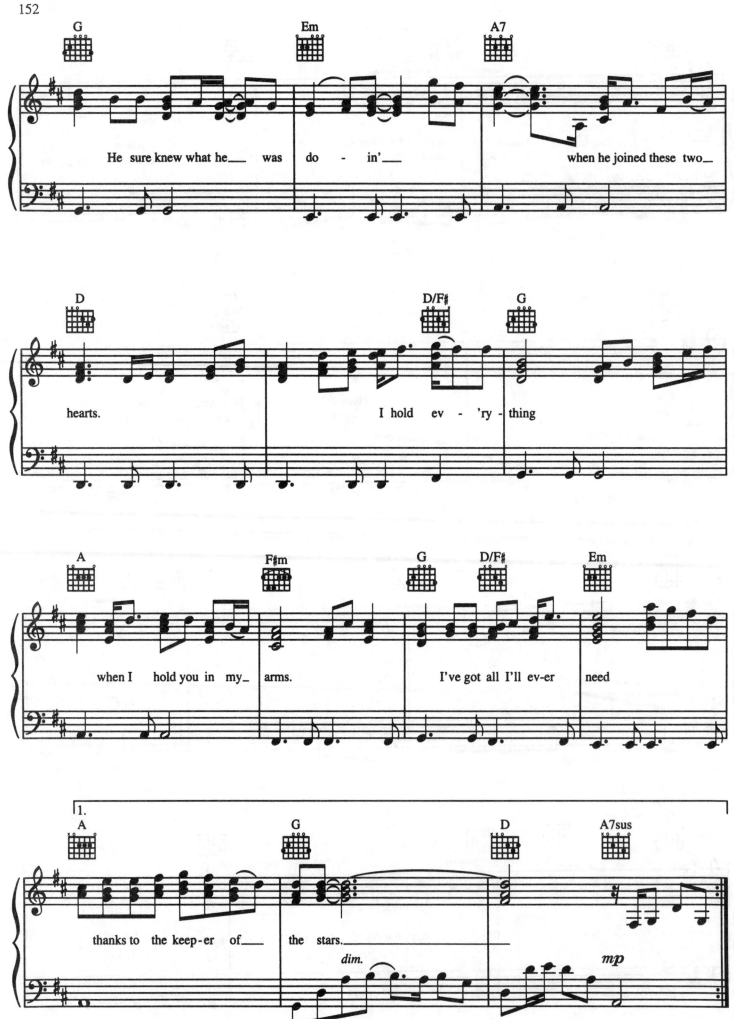

TO BE LOVED BY YOU

Words and Music by
MIKE REID and GARY BURR

% *Chorus:*

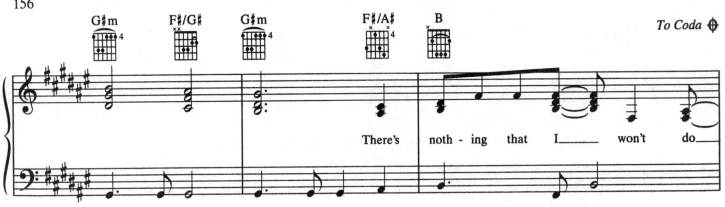

To Coda ⊕

There's noth-ing that I____ won't do____

to be loved by you.

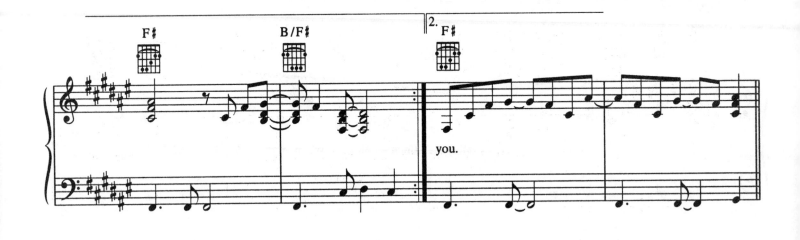

you.

Bridge:

E-ven when we're worlds____ a - part,____

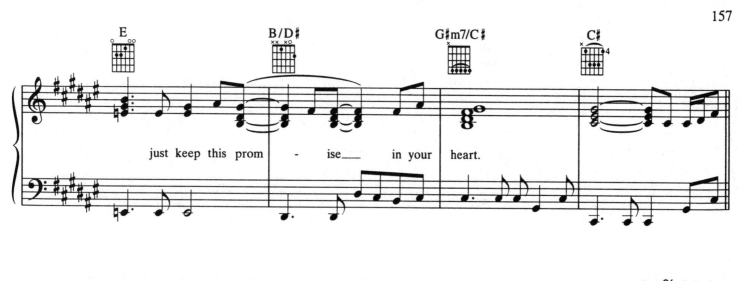

just keep this prom - ise___ in your heart.

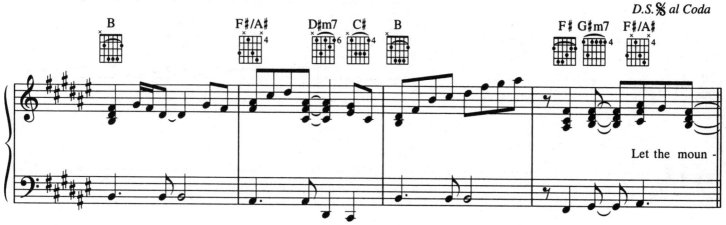

D.S. 𝄋 al Coda

Let the moun -

— there's noth-ing that I___ won't do,___ there's

noth-ing that I___ won't do___ to be loved by you.

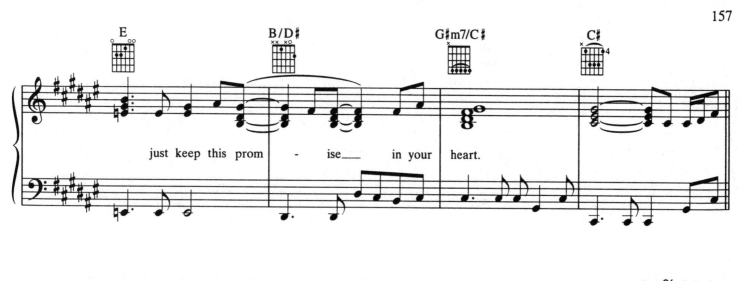

157

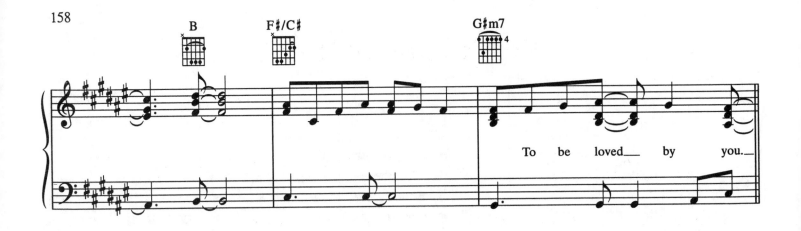

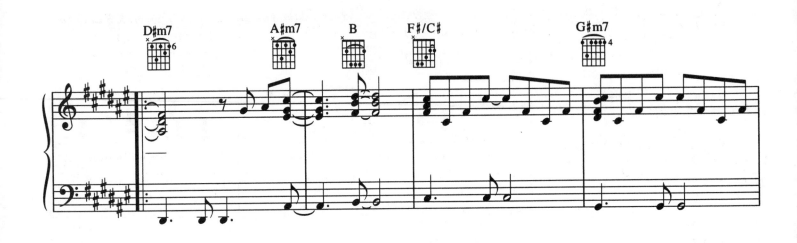

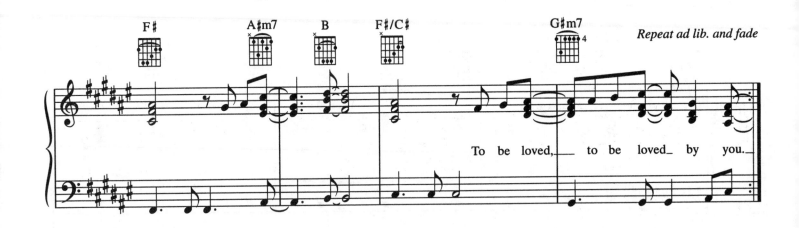

Verse 2:
There will be lonely nights
When you'll whisper my name.
Know, on those lonely nights,
I'll be doing the same.
Should every star in the sky go out,
Just keep your faith alive.
We were meant to be,
This is destiny,
It cannot be denied.
(To Chorus:)

YEARS FROM HERE

Words and Music by
GARY BAKER, JERRY WILLIAMS
and FRANK J. MYERS

Years from Here - 3 - 1

YOUR LOVE AMAZES ME

Words and Music by
CHUCK JONES and AMANDA HUNT

Verse 2:

I've seen a sunset that would make you cry,
And colors of a rainbow reaching 'cross the sky.
The moon in all its phases, but
Your love amazes me.
To Chorus:

Verse 3:

I've prayed for miracles that never came.
I got down on my knees in the pouring rain.
But only you could save me,
Your love amazes me.
(To Chorus:)

Standard Favorites

CAN'T TAKE MY EYES OFF OF YOU

Words and Music by
BOB CREWE and BOB GAUDIO

168

Can't Take My Eyes Off of You - 3 - 2

Can't Take My Eyes Off of You - 3 - 3

EVERYTHING I HAVE IS YOURS

Lyric by
HAROLD ADAMSON

Music by
BURTON LANE

Everything I Have Is Yours - 2 - 1

I ONLY HAVE EYES FOR YOU

Words by
AL DUBIN

Music by
HARRY WARREN

Are the Stars out to-night?__ I don't know if it's cloud-y or bright__ 'Cause I on-ly have eyes ____ for you, ____ dear. ____ The moon may be high, __ but I can't see a thing in the sky, __ 'Cause I on-ly have eyes ____ for you ____ I don't know if we're in a gar - den, __

I Only Have Eyes for You - 2 - 2

I WANNA BE LOVED BY YOU

Words by
BERT KALMAR

Music by
HERBERT STOTHART and HARRY RUBY

I Wanna Be Loved by You - 3 - 1

I Wanna Be Loved by You - 3 - 2

I Wanna Be Loved by You - 3 - 3

THE IRISH WEDDING SONG
(The Wedding Song)

Words and Music by
IAN BETTERIDGE

Moderate, gentle waltz

The Irish Wedding Song - 3 - 1

God bless this coup - le___ who mar - ry to - day.
God bless this fam - 'ly___ who start - ed to - day.
God bless this coup - le___ who mar - ry to - day.

Chorus

In good times and bad times, in sick - ness and

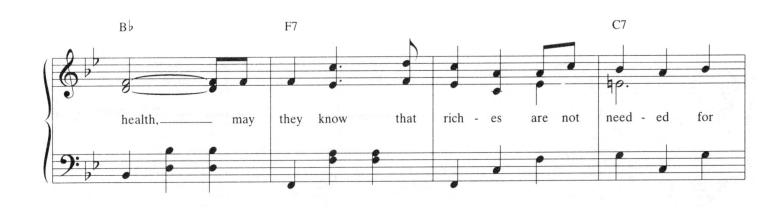

health,_____ may they know that rich - es are not need - ed for

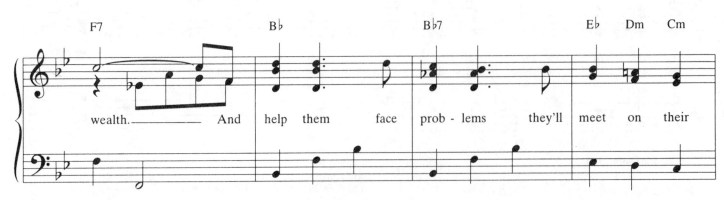

wealth._____ And help them face prob - lems they'll meet on their

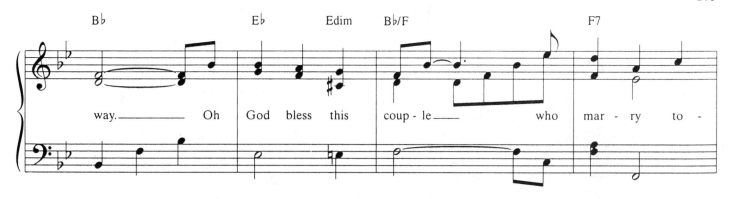

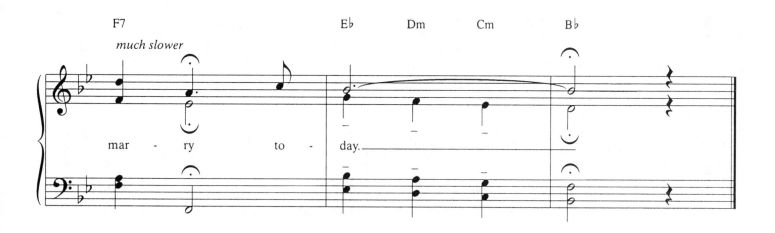

The Irish Wedding Song - 3 - 3

IT HAD TO BE YOU

Words by
GUS KAHN

Music by
ISHAM JONES

It Had to Be You - 3 - 1

It Had to Be You - 3 - 3

THE MORE I SEE YOU

Words by
MACK GORDON

Music by
HARRY WARREN

The More I See You - 3 - 1

184

The More I See You - 3 - 3

LET ME CALL YOU SWEETHEART

(I'm in Love with You)

Words by
BETH SLATER WHITSON

Music by
LEO FRIEDMAN

Let Me Call You Sweetheart - 2 - 1

LOVE AND MARRIAGE

Words by
SAMMY CAHN

Music by
JAMES VAN HEUSEN

LOVE AND MAR-RIAGE, LOVE AND MAR-RIAGE, Go to-geth-er like a horse and car-riage,

This I tell ya, broth-er, Ya can't have one with-out the oth-er.

LOVE AND MAR-RIAGE, LOVE AND MAR-RIAGE, It's an in-sti-tute you can't dis-par-age,

Ask the lo-cal gen-try And they will say it's el-e-men-t'ry. Try, try,

Love and Marriage - 2 - 2

LOVE ME WITH ALL YOUR HEART

English Lyric by
SUNNY SKYLAR
Spanish Lyric by
MARIO RIGUAL

Music by
CARLOS RIGUAL and
CARLOS ALBERTO MARTINOLI

Love Me With All Your Heart - 2 - 1

Love Me With All Your Heart - 2 - 2

Traditional Favorites

CUTTING THE CAKE
(The Farmer in the Dell)

TRADITIONAL
Arranged by PAMELA SCHULTZ

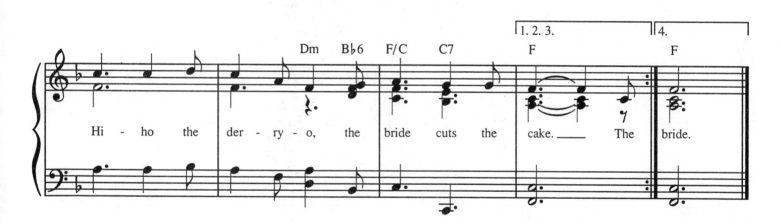

Verse 2:
The groom cuts the cake.
The groom cuts the cake.
Hi-ho the derry-o,
The groom cuts the cake.

Verse 3:
The bride feeds the groom.
The bride feeds the groom.
Hi-ho the derry-o,
The bride feeds the groom.

Verse 4:
The groom feeds the bride.
The groom feeds the bride.
Hi-ho the derry-o,
The groom feeds the bride.

HAVA NAGILA

TRADITIONAL

Hora Tempo - not too fast

Ha - vah ____ na - gi - lah, ha - vah ____ na - gi - lah,

Ha - vah ____ na - gi - lah, v' - nis - m' - cha.

Ha - vah ____ na - gi - lah, ha - vah ____ na - gi - lah,

Hava Nagila - 3 - 1

Ha - vah _____ na - gi - lah v' nis - m' - cha.

Ha - vah n' - ra - n' - nah, ha - vah n' - ra - 'n - nah,

Ha - vah n' - ra - n' - nah, v' - nis - m' - cha. cha.

U - ru u - ru a - chim, U - ru a - chim b' -

HEVENU SHALOM ALECHEM

TRADITIONAL
Arranged by PAMELA SCHULTZ

MACARENA

Words and Music by
ANTONIO ROMERO
and RAFAEL RUIZ

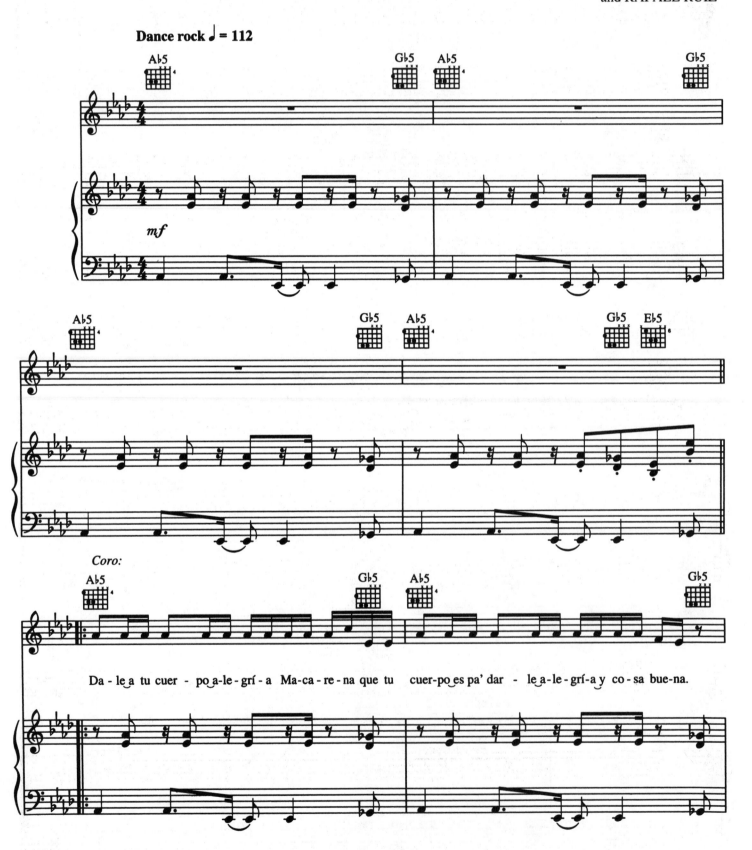

Coro:

Da - le a tu cuer - po a-le-grí - a Ma-ca-re-na que tu cuer-po es pa' dar - le a-le-grí-a y co-sa bue-na.

Macarena - 6 - 1

ju - ra de ban-de - ra del mu-cha-cho   se   la dió con dos a - mi-gos.   Ma-ca-

Puente:

re - na tie-ne un no-vio que se lla-ma,   que se   lla-ma de a-pe - lli - do Vi - to - ri - no   y en la

ju - ra de ban-de - ra del mu-cha-cho   se   la dió con dos a - mi-gos.

Coro:

Da - le a tu cuer - po a-le-grí - a Ma-ca - re - na que tu   cuer-po es pa' dar - le a-le-grí-a y co-sa bue-na.

Da - le a tu cuer - po a-le-grí - a Ma-ca - re - na, eh,_____ Ma - ca - re - na.

Da - le a tu cuer - po a-le-grí - a Ma-ca - re - na que tu cuer-po es pa' dar - le a-le-grí-a y co - sa bue-na.

Da - le a tu cuer - po a-le-grí - a Ma-ca - re - na, eh,_____ Ma - ca - re - na. 2. Ma-ca -

Versos 2 y 4:

re - na, Ma-ca - re - na, Ma-ca - re - na, que te gus-tan los ve - ra-nos de Mar-be - lla. Ma-ca -
4. *See additional lyric*

Da - le a tu cuer - po a - le - grí - a Ma - ca - re - na, eh,_____ Ma - ca - re - na.

Verso 3:
Macarena sueña con el Corte inglés
Y se compra los modelos mas modernos.
Le gustaría vivir en Nueva York
Y ligar un novio nuevo.

Puente 2:
Macarena sueña con el Corte inglés
Y se compra los modelos mas modernos.
Le gustaría vivir en Nueva York
Y ligar un novio nuevo.
(Al Coro:)

Verso 4:
Macarena tiene un novio que se llama,
Que se llama de apellido Vitorino.
Y en la jura de bandera del muchacho
Se la dió con dos amigos.

Puente 3:
Macarena tiene un novio que se llama,
Que se llama de apellido Vitorino.
Y en la jura de bandera del muchacho
Se la dió con dos amigos.
(Al Coro:)

REMOVING THE GARTER
(The Stripper)

By DAVID ROSE

Tempo di blues

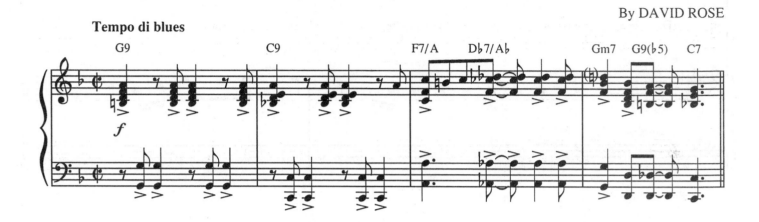

Chorus:

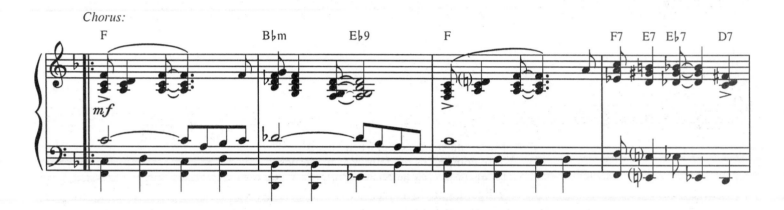

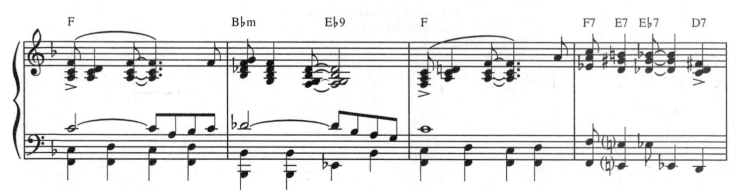

Removing the Garter - 2 - 1

TARANTELLA
(Italian Wedding Dance)

TRADITIONAL
Arranged by PAMELA SCHULTZ

Tarantella - 2 - 2

MEXICAN HAT DANCE

TRADITIONAL
Arranged by PAMELA SCHULTZ

Mexican Hat Dance - 3 - 1

Lyrics under the music:

hat. But its brim was not made just for danc - ing. It is

al - so quite good for ro - manc - ing, for my sweet-heart is al - ways en -

tranc - ing in his won - der - ful Mex - i - can hat.

Classical Favorites

AIR
(from the F Major Suite from ''Water Music'')

GEORGE FRIDERIC HANDEL

Adagio

Air - 2 - 1

AVE MARIA

(From the First Prelude of Johann Sebastian Bach)

Adapted by CHARLES GOUNOD

Andante con moto

tu - i Je - sus._____ Sanc - ta Ma -
God, the Lord most high!_____ Bless - ed Ma -

ri - a, sanc - ta Ma - ri - a, Ma -
ri - a! Bless - ed Ma - ri - a! Ma -

ri - a, o - ra___ pro - no - bis,
ri - a! Pray,_____ oh, pray__ for_____ us,

no - bis pec - ca - to - ri - bus,
for_____ us wretch - ed sin - ners,

BRIDAL CHORUS
(Wedding March from "Lohengrin")

RICHARD WAGNER

Andantino

Bridal Chorus - 4 - 1

Bridal Chorus - 4 - 2

Bridal Chorus - 4 - 4

AVE MARIA

FRANZ SCHUBERT, Op. 52

Ave Maria - 9 - 8

CANON IN D

JOHANN PACHELBEL (1653 - 1706)
Arranged for Piano by Robert Schultz

Canon in D - 9 - 1

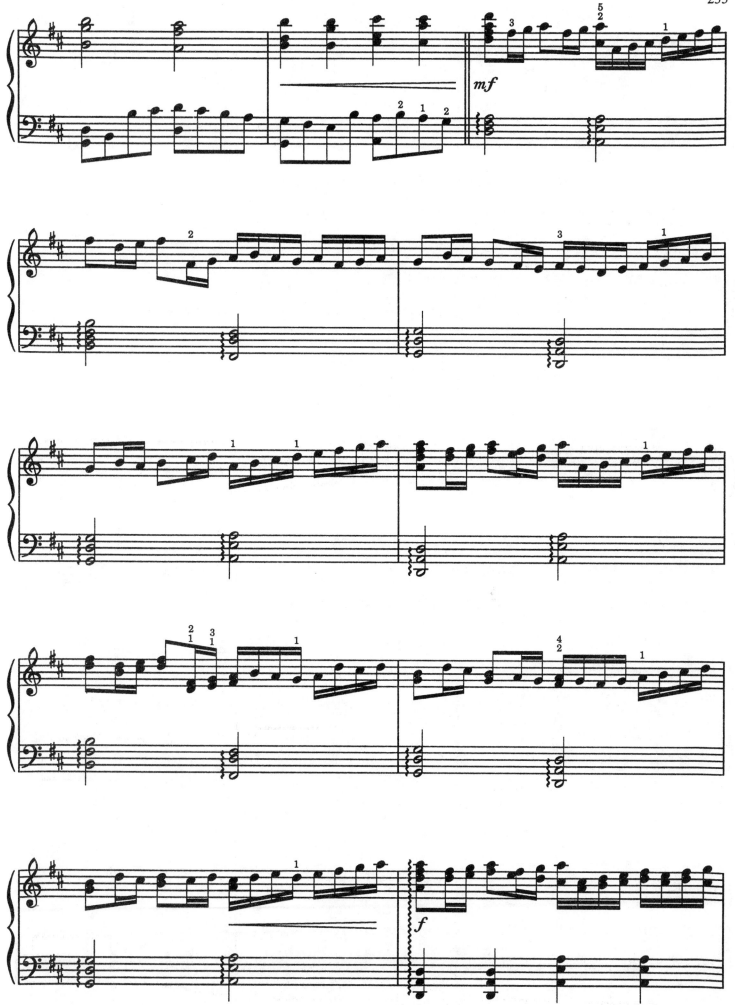

Canon in D - 9 - 3

Canon in D - 9 - 4

Canon in D - 9 - 5

Canon in D - 9 - 7

W·e·d·d·i·n·g M·u·s·i·c
from Warner Bros. Publications

♥ THE BEST OF POPULAR WEDDING MUSIC

Piano/Vocal/Chords (F3007SMB)
51 popular and standard titles appropriate for the wedding ceremony or the reception. Titles include: Always • Bridal Chorus (from Lohengrin) • Here and Now • Now and Forever (You and Me) • The Vows Go Unbroken (Always True To You) • Wedding March • You Are So Beautiful • You're the Inspiration.

♥ THE COMPLETE WEDDING MUSIC COLLECTION

Piano/Vocal/Chords (F3222SMB)
Easy Piano (F3222P2X)
A comprehensive collection. Ideal for the pianist who plays wedding services or receptions. Includes music which rarely appears in wedding publications, like Jewish wedding music, that is hard to find but is often requested. Includes: Ave Maria (Schubert) • Hava Nagila • Here and Now and more.

♥ FAVORITE WEDDING CLASSICS

Flute (F3228FLX)
Clarinet (F3228CLX)
Alto Sax (F3228ASX)
Trumpet (F3228TRX)
Piano Accompaniment (F3228PAX)
15 intermediate to advanced level arrangements by Keith Snell of the most often requested classical pieces for weddings. These can be played as solos, duets or trios with or without piano accompaniment. Includes "Air" (from Water Music - Handel) • Ave Maria (Gounod/J. S. Bach) • Bridal Chorus (from Lohengrin - Wagner).

♥ FOREVER . . . I DO
A Collection of Popular Music for Your Wedding Day

Piano/Vocal/Chords (F2510SMC)
Titles include: Cherish • Now and Forever (You and Me) • Always • I Won't Last a Day Without You • My Girl • We've Only Just Begun • Theme from Ice Castles (Through the Eyes of Love) and more.

♥ LOVE ALWAYS . . .

Piano/Vocal/Chords (F2942SMC)
Easy Piano (F2942P2X)
18 beautiful love songs, including: Always and Forever • Colour My World • Here and Now • The Vows Go Unbroken (Always True to You) • You Are So Beautiful.

♥ THE NEW BOOK OF GOLDEN WEDDING SONGS

Piano/Vocal/Chords (F2265SMB)
A perennial favorite, including more than 40 songs such as: And I Love You So • Because • Bridal Chorus (Lohengrin) • O Perfect Love • What Are You Doing the Rest of Your Life and more.

♥ POPULAR LOVE SONGS
Advanced Piano Library, Volume 1

(F2795P1D)
17 popular love songs arranged for advanced piano by Tom Roed. This spiral-bound folio is perfect for weddings and receptions. Titles include: Baby, Come to Me • The Greatest Love of All • On the Wings of Love • We've Only Just Begun • You Are So Beautiful.

♥ THE WEDDING COLLECTION

Easy Piano (F3279P2X)
12 popular and traditional songs including: Always and Forever • Ave Maria (Schubert) • In This Life • Now and Forever (You and Me) • You and I.

♥ THE WEDDING FAKEBOOK

C Edition (F3101FBX)
Bb Edition (F3102FBX)
Eb Edition (F3103FBX)
Over 159 traditional and popular songs in three matching spiral-bound editions. Includes: Always • Bridal Chorus (from Lohengrin) • Forever I Do (The Wedding Song) • Jesu, Joy of Man's Desiring • Now and Forever (You and Me) • Truly • Wedding March (Mendelssohn).

♥ A WEDDING PRESENT

Piano/Vocal/Chords (TMF0105D)
A treasury of 94 traditional, standard and popular songs including: The Way He Makes Me Feel • Colour My World • Today • I Just Called to Say I Love You • Bridal Chorus and more.

♥ WEDDING SHOWSTOPPERS

Piano/Vocal/Chords (F3298SMA)
94 titles including: After All (Love Theme from Chances Are) • Always • Forever I Do (The Wedding Song) • Forever's as Far as I'll Go • Here and Now • I Will Always Love You • Now and Forever (You and Me) • A Time for Us (Love Theme from Romeo and Juliet) • Up Where We Belong • You and I.

♥ WITH MY LOVE

Organ (TAO0104)
This collection contains 55 songs of love, including: Friendly Persuasion • I Love You Truly • My Blue Heaven • The Shadow of Your Smile • Through the Years • A Time for Us (Love Theme from Romeo and Juliet) and more.

♥ THE WORLD'S BEST LOVED WEDDING MUSIC

Piano/Vocal/Chords (F2431SMX)
Titles include: Always and Forever • Ave Maria • Bridal Chorus (Wedding March from Lohengrin) • I Honestly Love You • Liebestraum • Love Story • Processional and We've Only Just Begun.